Nelson

Handwriting

Copymasters

for Book A

CM		Pupil Book A Unit	
1	S	1	
2	S	1	Handwriting patterns
3	S	1	
4	S	2	
5	S	2	
6	S	2	Revision of the unjoined script
7	S	2	
8	E	2	
9	E	2	
10	S	3	The joined script; cursive **f** and **k**
11	S	4	
12	E	4	
13	S	4	
14	E	4	
15	S	4	
16	E	4	The first join
17	S	4	
18	E	4	
19	S	4	
20	E	4	
21	S	4	
22	E	4	
23	S	5	
24	E	5	
25	S	5	
26	E	5	
27	S	5	The second join
28	E	5	
29	S	5	
30	E	5	
31	S	6	
32	E	6	
33	S	6	
34	E	6	The third join
35	S	6	
36	E	6	
37	S	6	
38	E	6	

CM		Pupil Book A Unit	
39	S	7	
40	E	7	The fourth join
41	S	7	
42	E	7	
43	S	8	The break letters
44	E	8	
45	S	9	
46	E	9	Capital letters
47	E	9	
48	S	10	
49	S	10	
50	S	10	
51	S	10	Revision of the four joins
52	E	10	
53	E	10	
54	E	10	
55	S	11	
56	S	11	Practice with poems and party invitations
57	E	11	
58	E	11	
59		12	Check your writing
60		12	
61			Assessment Sheet 1
62			Assessment Sheet 2
63			Practice Sheet

Nelson

Handwriting patterns

Name

Go over the loops.

Pupil Book A Unit 1   pages 2-3 Support Copymaster

Handwriting patterns

Name

Go over the clouds and the parachute.

Pupil Book A Unit 1 pages 2-3 Support Copymaster

Nelson Handwriting

Handwriting patterns

Name

Go over the patterns.

Pupil Book A   Unit 1   pages 2-3   Support Copymaster

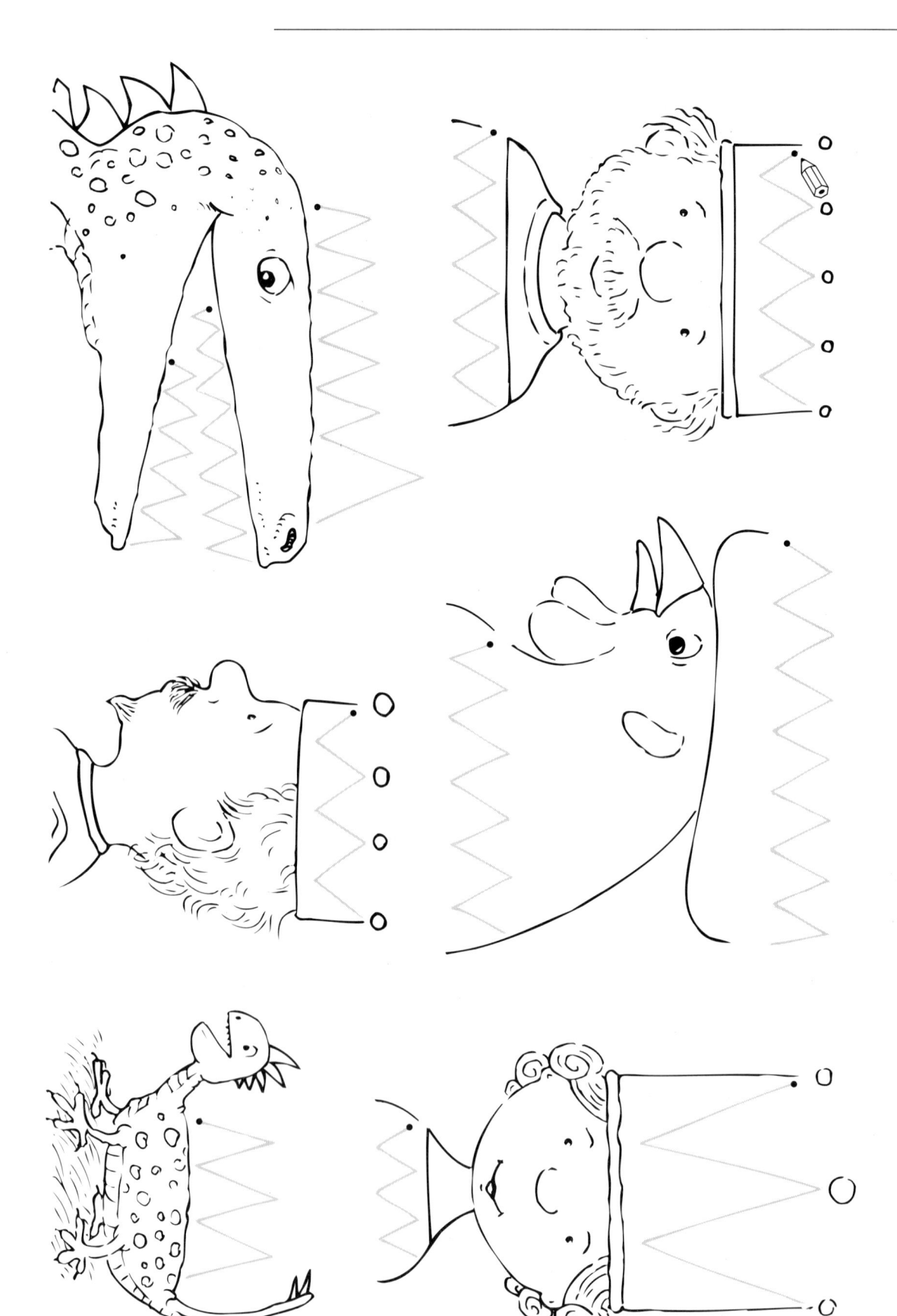

Nelson Handwriting

Revision of the unjoined script

Name

	a	A
	b	B
	c	C
	d	D
	e	E
	f	F
	g	G
	h	H
	i	I

Pupil Book A Unit 2 pages 4–5 Support Copymaster

Nelson Handwriting

Revision of the unjoined script

Name

j j   J J
k k   K K
l l   L L
m m   M M
n n   N N
o o   O O
p p   P P
q q   Q Q
r r   R R

Pupil Book A Unit 2 pages 4-5 Support Copymaster

Nelson Handwriting

Revision of the unjoined script

Name

s S
t T
u U
v V
w W
x X
y Y
z Z

Pupil Book A Unit 2 pages 4-5 Support Copymaster

Nelson Handwriting

Revision of the unjoined script

Name

0 0
1 1
2 2
3 3
4 4
5 5
6 6
7 7
8 8
9 9

Pupil Book A   Unit 2   pages 4-5   Support Copymaster

Nelson Handwriting

Revision of the unjoined script

Name _____

Copy this sentence.

Robert and his puppy

R

run through puddles.

r

Now copy the sentence again.

Pupil Book A Unit 2 pages 4–5 Extension Copymaster

Nelson Handwriting

Revision of the unjoined script

Name

Copy this sentence.

Snails and tortoises

s

always move slowly.

a

Now copy the sentence again.

Pupil Book A Unit 2 pages 4-5 Extension Copymaster

Nelson Handwriting

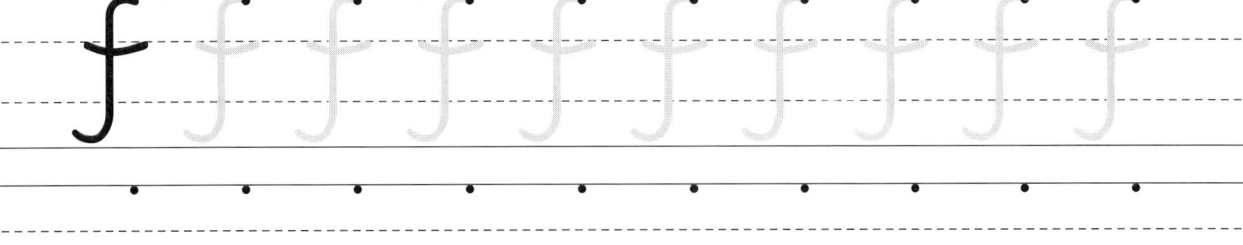

The joined script; cursive f and k

Name ....

f — fish

f f f f f f f f f f

k — king

k k k k k k k k k k

Pupil Book A Unit 3 pages 6–7 Support Copymaster

Nelson Handwriting

The first join

Name

in in in in in in

in in

in in in in in in

in in

Pupil Book A Unit 4 pages 8-9 Support Copymaster

Nelson Handwriting

The first join

Name

in

bin

din

fin

pin

tin

win

Pupil Book A   Unit 4   pages 8-9   Extension Copymaster

Nelson Handwriting

The first join

Name

in im ig

in

din

im

dim

ig

dig

Pupil Book A Unit 4 pages 10-11 Support Copymaster

Nelson Handwriting

The first join

Name _____

ni   ni   nine

mi   mi   mice

hi   hi   hide

li   li   lid

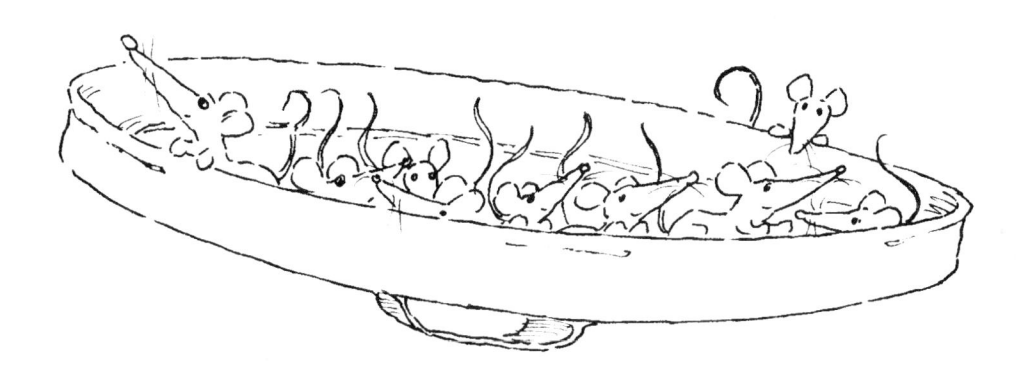

Nine mice hide in a lid.

N

Pupil Book A Unit 4 pages 10–11 Extension Copymaster

Nelson Handwriting

The first join

Name

ud un up

ud *ud*

mud *mud*

un *un*

bun *bun*

up *up*

cup *cup*

Pupil Book A Unit 4 pages 12-13 Support Copymaster

Nelson Handwriting

The first join

Name _____

di *di*   dig

mu *mu*   mud

hu *hu*   hug

tu *tu*   tub

a dig in the mud

a

a hug in the tub

a

Pupil Book A Unit 4 pages 12–13 Extension Copymaster

Nelson Handwriting

The first join

Name

em eg ee

em

hem

eg

leg

ee

eel

Pupil Book A Unit 4 pages 14-15 Support Copymaster

Nelson Handwriting

The first join

Name _____

he   *he*   hen

de   *de*   made

ce   *ce*   nice

ke   *ke*   cake

The hen made a nice cake.

Pupil Book A Unit 4 pages 14-15 Extension Copymaster

Nelson Handwriting

The first join

Name

ag   am   ap

ag
tag
am
jam
ap
cap

Pupil Book A Unit 4 pages 16-17 Support Copymaster

Nelson Handwriting

The first join

Name

ma *ma*   man

ca *ca*   car

ha *ha*   hand

na *na*   nail

a man in a car

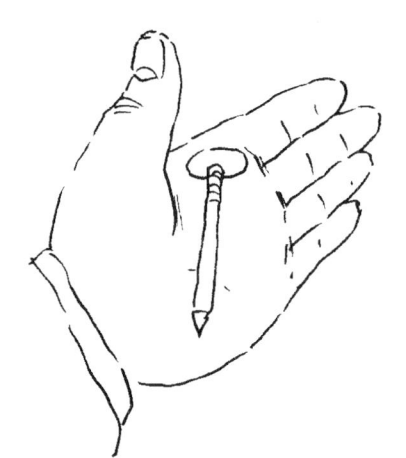

a

a nail in my hand

a

Pupil Book A Unit 4 pages 16-17 Extension Copymaster

Nelson Handwriting

The first join

Name

si   **sa**   **su**

si   si

sit   sit

sa   sa

sad   sad

su   su

sun   sun

Pupil Book A   Unit 4   pages 18-19   Support Copymaster

Nelson Handwriting

The first join

Name

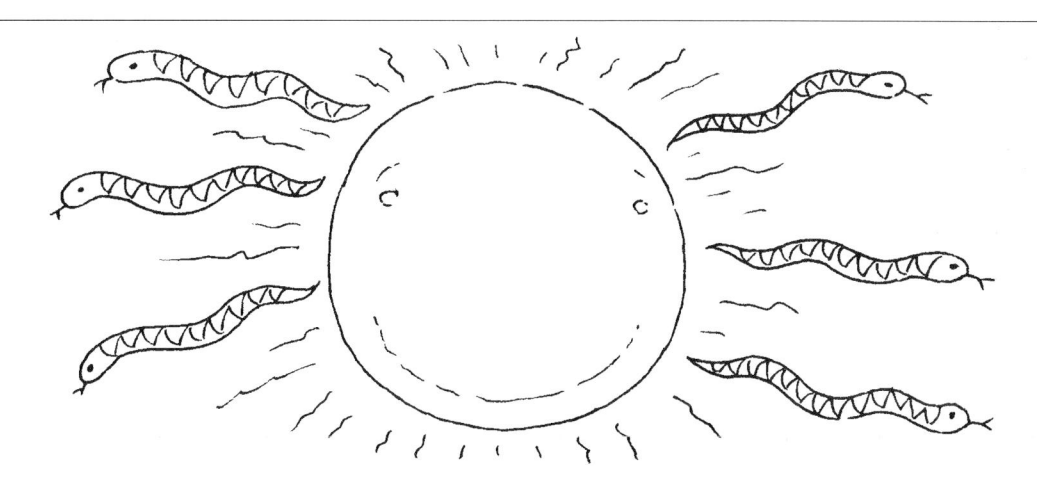

se · *se* · see
si · *si* · six
sn · *sn* · snake
su · *su* · sun

I see six snakes in the sun.

Pupil Book A Unit 4 pages 18-19 Extension Copymaster

Nelson Handwriting

The second join

Name

ill   ib   it

ill   ill

till   till

ib   ib

nib   nib

it   it

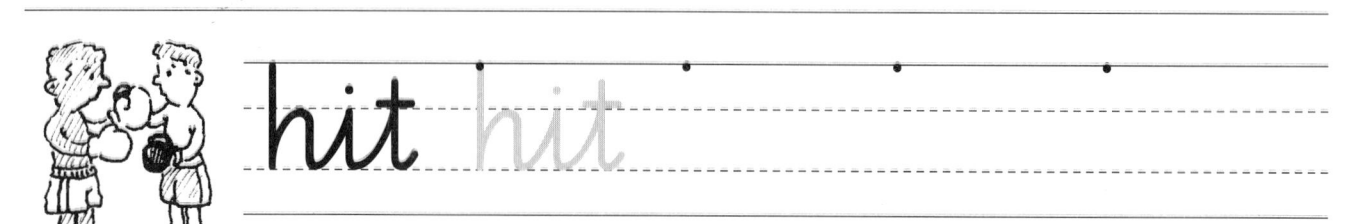

hit   hit

Pupil Book A Unit 5 pages 20-21 Support Copymaster

Nelson Handwriting

The second join

Name

ike   ike   like

it   it   sit

ill   ill   still

ile   ile   smile

I like to sit still and smile.

Pupil Book A Unit 5 pages 20-21 Extension Copymaster

Nelson Handwriting

The second join

Name _____

ack **uck** **eck**

ack

sack

uck

duck

eck

neck

Pupil Book A Unit 5 pages 22-23 Support Copymaster

Nelson Handwriting

The second join

Name

nt   nt   ant

nk   nk   sink

cl   cl   clap

ck   ck   back

an ant in a sink

a

a clap on the back

a

Pupil Book A Unit 5 pages 22-23 Extension Copymaster

Nelson Handwriting

The second join

Name

ch sh th

ch ch

chin chin

sh sh

ship ship

th th

thin thin

Pupil Book A Unit 5 pages 24-25 Support Copymaster

Nelson Handwriting

The second join

Name

ch ch chimp

itch itch ditch

th th thin

sh sh sheep

a chimp in a ditch

a

a thin sheep

a

Pupil Book A   Unit 5   pages 24-25   Extension Copymaster

The second join

Name

it   ut   lf

it

hit

ut

cut

lf

shelf

Pupil Book A Unit 5 pages 26-27 Support Copymaster

Nelson Handwriting

The second join

Name

it · *it* · hit

ett · *ett* · better

nt · *nt* · tent

if · *if* · lift

A tent is better if it rains.

A

Pupil Book A Unit 5 pages 26-27 Extension Copymaster

Nelson Handwriting

The third join

Name

ock   op   one

ock

clock

op

hop

one

stone

Pupil Book A   Unit 6   pages 28-29   Support Copymaster

Nelson Handwriting

The third join

Name

ou   ou   our

oa   oa   coat

oo   oo   hook

om   om   home

Hang your coat on a hook.

H

Pupil Book A Unit 6 pages 28-29 Extension Copymaster

Nelson Handwriting

The third join

Name

fa ra va

fa

fat

ra

rat

va

vat

Pupil Book A Unit 6 pages 30-31 Support Copymaster

Nelson Handwriting

The third join

Name

fo   four

fi   fish

wi   wig

wo   worm

four fat fish

a worm in a wig

Pupil Book A Unit 6 pages 30-31 Extension Copymaster

Nelson Handwriting

The third join

Name _____

fe we re

fe *fe*

fell *fell*

we *we*

well *well*

re *re*

read *read*

Pupil Book A Unit 6 pages 32-33 Support Copymaster

Nelson Handwriting

The third join

Name

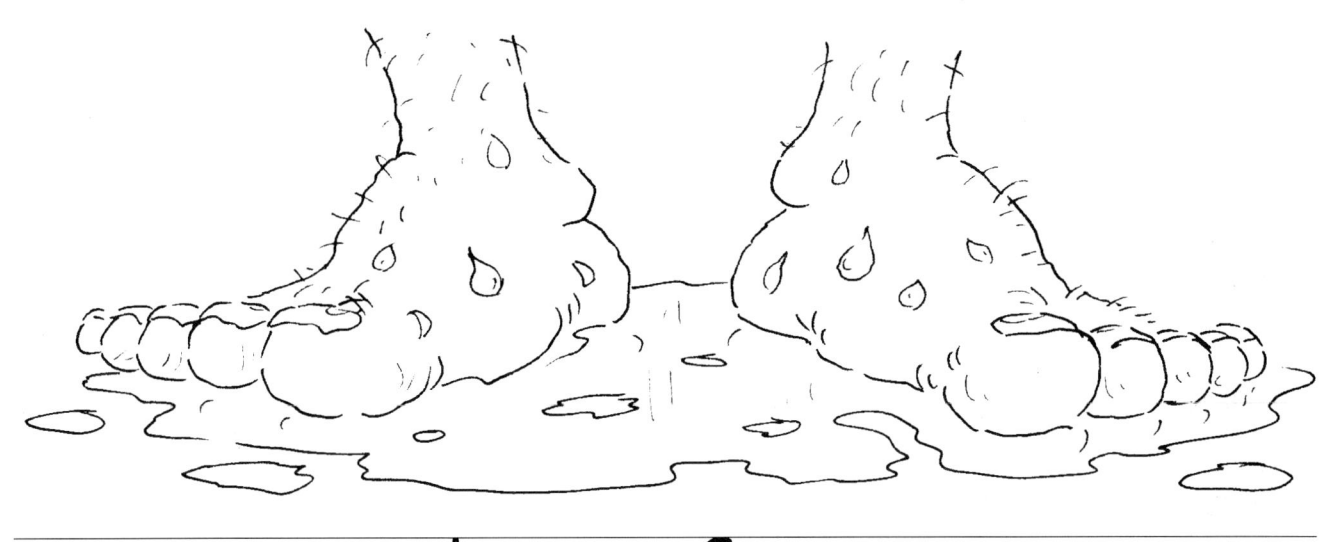

we   wet

ve   very

re   tired

fe   feet

very tired wet feet

Pupil Book A Unit 6 pages 32-33 Extension Copymaster

Nelson Handwriting

The third join

Name

ws   rs   os

ws

cows

rs

cars

os

lost

Pupil Book A   Unit 6   pages 34–35   Support Copymaster

Nelson Handwriting

The third join

Name _____

os   os   ghost

orse orse   horse

rs   rs   jars

ws   ws   screws

a ghost on a horse

a

jars and screws

j

Pupil Book A Unit 6 pages 34–35 Extension Copymaster

Nelson Handwriting

The fourth join

Name

old oke ot

old

cold

oke

smoke

ot

slot

Pupil Book A Unit 7 pages 36-37 Support Copymaster

Nelson Handwriting

The fourth join

Name

ot ot	hot
of of	often
old old	old
obe obe	robe

I get hot in my old robe.

Pupil Book A   Unit 7   pages 36-37   Extension Copymaster

Nelson Handwriting

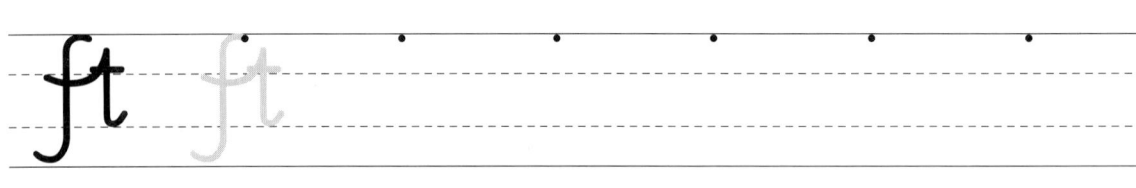

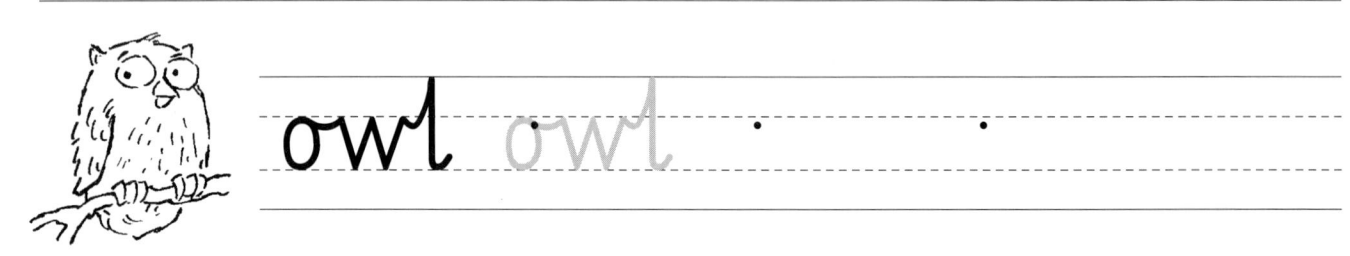

The fourth join

Name

ft rt wt

ft

loft

rt

fort

wt

owl

Pupil Book A Unit 7 pages 38-39 Support Copymaster

Nelson Handwriting

The fourth join

Name _____

ark *ark*   bark

owl *owl*   growl

iff *iff*   sniff

ort *ort*   snort

bark and growl

b

sniff and snort

s

Pupil Book A   Unit 7   pages 38-39 Extension Copymaster

Nelson Handwriting

The break letters

Name

- baby
- girl
- jump
- play
- queen
- foxes
- yacht
- zebra

Pupil Book A Unit 8 pages 40-41 Support Copymaster

Nelson Handwriting

The break letters

Name

a baby in a bubble bath

a

a girl in a garage

a

people jumping in a jeep

p

a queen eating yogurt

a

foxes and zebras in a zoo

f

Pupil Book A   Unit 8   pages 40-41   Extension Copymaster

Nelson Handwriting

Capital letters

Name _____

Use a capital letter at the beginning of each sentence and at the beginning of each person's name.

My name is _____

M

My friend's name is _____

M

My teacher's name is _____

M

Hello. My name is Ben. What is your name?

Pupil Book A   Unit 9   pages 42–43   Support Copymaster

Capital letters

Name

Copy these signs.
Use capital letters.

ROAD

EXIT

SALE

NO ENTRY

WAY IN

CAR PARK

SCHOOL

Capital letters

Name _____

Choose one of these slogans.
Design a poster and write the slogan in capital letters.
Decorate the poster with a picture.

- eat more fruit
- take lots of exercise
- keep yourself clean
- go to bed early
- brush your teeth well
- eat fresh vegetables

Pupil Book A Unit 9 pages 42-43 Extension Copymaster

Revision of the four joins

Name

all chair chip

duck into kick

like make much

that the then

Pupil Book A Unit 10 pages 44-45 Support Copymaster

Nelson Handwriting

Revision of the four joins

Name

animal called

cat chicken little

lunch talked teeth

their thinking under

Pupil Book A Unit 10 pages 44-45 Support Copymaster

Nelson Handwriting

Revision of the four joins

Name _____

are down for

have how looked

odd old on out

owl told took

Pupil Book A Unit 10 pages 44–45 Support Copymaster

Revision of the four joins

Name

warm   web   went

were   what   when

where   which   white

who   why

Pupil Book A   Unit 10   pages 44–45   Support Copymaster

Nelson Handwriting

Revision of the four joins

Name

eyes

ears

nose

lips

hair

face

Pupil Book A   Unit 10   pages 44–45   Extension Copymaster

Nelson Handwriting

Revision of the four joins

Name

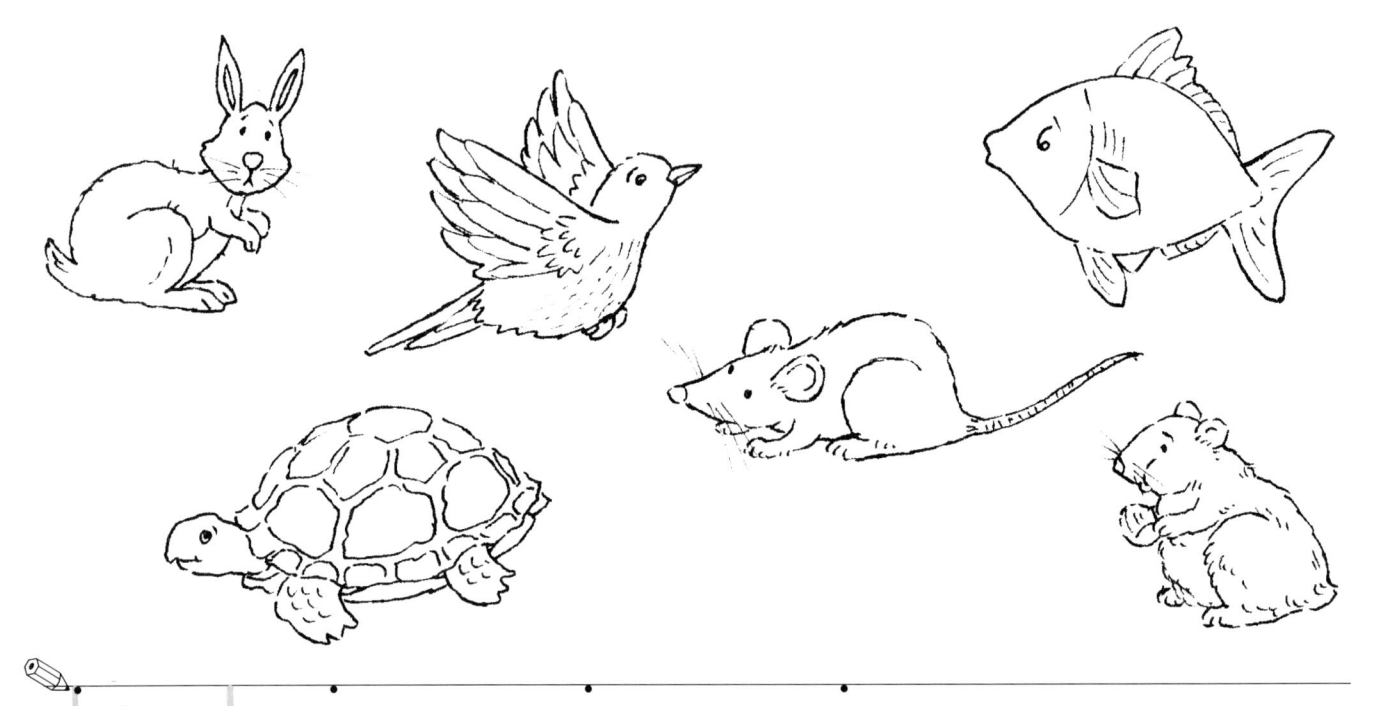

bird

fish

mouse

rabbit

hamster

tortoise

Pupil Book A . Unit 10 pages 44-45 Extension Copymaster

Nelson Handwriting

Revision of the four joins

Name

mum

mummy

mother

dad

daddy

father

sister

brother

baby

Pupil Book A Unit 10 pages 44-45 Extension Copymaster

Nelson Handwriting

Practice with poems and party invitations

Name

Copy this poem carefully into your book.

Mix a pancake,

Stir a pancake,

Pop it in the pan,

Fry the pancake,

Toss the pancake,

Catch it if you can.

Pupil Book A   Unit 11   pages 46-47   Support Copymaster

Nelson Handwriting

Practice with poems and party invitations

Name

Copy Sam's party menu.

Cheese and pineapple

C

Sausages on sticks

S

Slices of pizza

S

Fruit jelly

F

Pupil Book A Unit 11 pages 46-47 Support Copymaster

Nelson Handwriting

Practice with poems and party invitations

Name _____

Make a neat copy of this poem in your book.

Cariad Bach, O Cariad Bach
Shall you sing to the moon?
Shall you shout for the dark?
Shall you whisper with bears?
Shall you waken the night?
O Cariad Bach, soft dreams
And sleep tight.

Pupil Book A Unit 11 pages 46-47 Extension Copymaster

Nelson Handwriting

Practice with poems and party invitations

Name _____

Copy these rules for playing "Pass the parcel" into your book.

Sit in a circle.

Play some music.

Pass the parcel around.

When the music stops,

take one wrapper off the parcel.

The person who takes the last

wrapper off the parcel wins the prize.

Pupil Book A   Unit II   pages 46-47   Extension Copymaster

Nelson Handwriting

Check your writing

Name

Copy these words in your best handwriting.

tin can lap meet

seat slab dull chick

hard wood fire cows

old loft howl dark

Pupil Book A   Unit 12   page 48

Nelson Handwriting

Check your writing

Name

Copy this sentence in your best handwriting.

Five or six big jet planes zoomed quickly by the new tower.

Describe your favourite toy.
Say what you like about it.
Use your best handwriting.

Pupil Book A   Unit 12   page 48

Nelson Handwriting

Assessment Sheet (1)
for Nelson Handwriting Books A, 1, 2, 3, 4

Child's name _____

Date of birth _____ Right/left-handed _____

Tick or date entries to record the child's achievement of each skill.

1 Writing habits
Does the child: **Comments**

a) sit comfortably and correctly? ☐ _____

b) hold the pencil in an appropriate tripod grip? ☐ _____

c) position the paper correctly? ☐ _____

d) make pencil strokes smoothly and without undue pressure? ☐ _____

2 Basic letter patterns
Can the child make the following patterns rhythmically and easily?

a) straight lines |||–––|||–– ☐ _____

b) diagonals   wwwww ☐ _____

c) pulls or swings   uuuuu ☐ _____

d) pushes or bridges   nnnnn ☐ _____

e) spirals   eeeee ☐ _____

f) c pattern   ccccc ☐ _____

3 Construction of letters
Complete the table below.

a) Are the letters made with the correct movements? ☐ _____

b) Are all the letters except f, i, j, t, x made without lifting pencil from paper? ☐ _____

c) Are downstrokes vertical and parallel or sloping slightly to the right? ☐ _____

d) Do a, b, c, d, e, g, o, p, q have oval rather than rounded bodies? ☐ _____

e) Are the letters correct in shape and proportion? ☐ _____

	a	b	c	d	e	f	g	h	i	j	k	l	m	n	o	p	q	r	s	t	u	v	w	x	y	z
a)																										
b)																										
c)																										
d)																										
e)																										

Pupil Book A   Assessment Copymaster

Nelson Handwriting

Assessment Sheet (2)
for Nelson Handwriting Books A, 1, 2, 3, 4

Child's name _____

Date of birth _____ Right/left-handed _____

Tick or date entries to record the child's achievement of each skill.

4 Size of writing   **Comments**

a) Is the size of writing appropriate? ☐ _____

b) Are the letters regular in size? ☐ _____

c) Are the relative heights and proportions of the different types of letter correct? ☐ _____

5 Spacing of letters, words and lines

a) Does the space between letters appear uniform? ☐ _____

b) Is the space between words regular and appropriate? ☐ _____

c) Is the space between lines regular and appropriate? ☐ _____

d) Is the writing correctly aligned across the page? ☐ _____

6 Joined writing (Beginning stage)
Can the child do the following:

a) Perform the swings pattern confidently? ☐ _____

b) Make the joins correctly and as continuous movements:

    the first join?   *in* ☐ _____

    the second join?   *ab* ☐ _____

    the third join?   *oc* ☐ _____

    the fourth join?   *ob* ☐ _____

c) Use the break letters appropriately and with regular spacing? ☐ _____

d) Use the different forms of s and e appropriately? ☐ _____

7 Joined writing (Mastery stage)

a) Has the size of writing decreased appropriately? ☐ _____

b) Is the writing upright or with a regular slope of not more than 8° to the right? ☐ _____

c) Can the child evaluate his/her writing competently? ☐ _____

d) Is the writing free of the faults listed below?

    Letters too short or too tall ☐ _____

    Letters with their tails too long or too curly ☐ _____

    Badly made joins ☐ _____

    Downstrokes not all in the same direction ☐ _____

    Cross-strokes of f or t in the wrong place ☐ _____

    Dot of i or j missed out or in the wrong place ☐ _____

    Wrong spacing between letters, words or lines ☐ _____

    Writing not straight across the page ☐ _____

Pupil Book A   Assessment Copymaster

Nelson Handwriting

Practice sheet

Name

Pupil Book A Practice Sheet